Poems, Lyrics and Thoughts

A series of short poems some that could be adapted as lyrics and interesting thoughts to keep you amused and thinking.

Herbie Dunnan

authorHOUSE®

AuthorHouse™ UK
1663 Liberty Drive
Bloomington, IN 47403 USA
www.authorhouse.co.uk
Phone: 0800.197.4150

Published by AuthorHouse 04/04/2018

ISBN: 978-1-5462-9066-7 (sc)
ISBN: 978-1-5462-9065-0 (e)

Print information available on the last page.

This book is printed on acid-free paper.

Contents

Acknowledgements

I would like to take this opportunity to thank you all;
My family, friends and colleagues
You have believed in me and encouraged
me to get going and make a start,
Without you telling me I could do this; I
really don't think I would even have
Looked into the procedures of starting
to get my words published
Thank you!
Dino and **Sinclair,** my longest and oldest
friends since I have lived in England
Friends from time Friends for life
Nuff Respect
Special Thanks and Appreciation
Kerry My niece (centrepiececakesbykerry.co.uk)
You started your own business and doing well
This has also given me an enormous push forward
To do my own thing
Big up u status
Cousin Nora when have you not been there for me?
See I've done it – *Thank you!*

Sanndeo Purgass

Thank you for your Illustrations and technical input
Very much appreciated

Carolyn

Because we're together anything is possible
Love you long time

Dedications

This book is dedicated to my
beloved Mother and Father
For loving me and showing me the right from wrong
Throughout my life until their passing;
may they forever rest in peace
Even when I thought they were wrong
deep in my subconscious
I knew they were always right
RIP Mama and Dada

Carolyn

I think of you all the time and how things could be
I think of us being together for eternity

I dream of you late at night and think of you at dawn
And I wish we were together on a sunny summer morn

I love the way you carry yourself a princess yes you are
If not then you must, be a super star

I hear your voice on the phone and think it's really sad
That you're so near yet far away; baby that's bad

I get up every morning and pray for everything,
And wish you were here my darling Carolyn.

My Thoughts

If I was famous would my daughter want to know?
If I was an artist would she come to my show?
If I was a millionaire would she care then?
Would she be happy and tell all her friends?

Would she google my name and say that's my dad?
Or do you think she'd forget me like she has? That's sad.
Should I have fought tooth and nail
like her mother wanted?
Or was I wrong to stay humble and placid?

These are the questions I ask myself,
I haven't got no answers; only she can tell

You're a big woman now and you should
have a mind of your own,
I think you are living in a twilight zone.

My name is on the paper no matter what you call yourself,
I know I'm rich; love is my wealth.

My grandchildren what do they say?
They don't even know me; or give me the time of
day, I'm hurting inside but I don't really ponder,
Do you know I love you all? Hmmm I wonder.
Where did I go wrong, what did I do?
It really doesn't help when you say it's not me it's you.

A Fathers Lament For His Child

Why does a mother take a child from a Father?
Then pretend he doesn't exist
How can a Mother poison a Childs
mind (against the Father?)
Just to live her life in bliss

What happens to the child when the child grows?
Now the child mind is infested
The child stops caring; becomes insincere
Because of what has been injected.

Your child has children, you're a Granddad
But you're not allowed to see them
So the grandchildren grows and don't even know
That you care and you want to see them.

You think what have I done; to be excluded from the fun?
You scratch your head and ponder
Should you make more calls or knock at the door?
Would it cause more trouble? I wonder.

What is so important on your phone?

What you goanna do when your kid is lying
Stretched out on the tarmac?
I know you'll be crying.

You texting while crossing the road
They are your children
Don't try to offload.

Using your phone can wait
look after your children's welfare state.
What's so important on your phone?
If your child gets knocked,
You goanna to start moan.

What's so important on your phone?
Why let your children walk
In a danger zone?

Do you really need to be using?
This is a form of abusing.
What's so important on your phone?
Why can't you just leave it alone?

Tottenham Riot

It was a sad day in Tottenham
When someone lit that flame
It was a sad sad day in Tottenham
And the black man got the blame.

They said the unemployed caused the riots
And they were mostly black
But I tell you they've got it wrong
Cos that is not the facts

They say the shooting of Mark Duggan
Upset the apple cart
But I don't believe they know for sure
How the whole thing start.

But burning and looting that is really bad
Don't let it happen again cos that would
Be so sad

From all kind of violence we must all refrain
Live together in peace let's stop all the pain

It was a sad sad day in Tottenham
Is it bubbling up again?
They said lawful killing
And it's causing the family pain

Where's the mini cab driver? I haven't
seen him on the news
Where's the box the gun was in
Are they sure it wasn't just shoes?

The guy that took the video from the block,
What's happened to him? Is he also
Lying on his back?

It was a sad day in Tottenham
When someone lit the flame,
It was a sad sad day in Tottenham
And t the black man got the blame.

Shakespeare Dead

To be or not to be? That is what Shakespeare asked
But it seems **our** history has been left in the dark.

It's hardly mentioned, it's like we have no past
But our history is deep, in fact it is quite vast

Shakespeare wrote plays that we all remember
In schools, they teach this from January to December
He wrote Macbeth, Othello, and Hamlet,
he also wrote the tempest
Romeo and Juliet.

We know this because it is there in our face,
Why don't they teach **OUR** history? I think it is a disgrace

Is our history even; sitting on their shelves?
I know Shakespeare's books are,
Gathering them wealth.
I'm not upset; not unhappy at all,
it's just that were still little
While Shakespeare's so tall

What is obvious? They need to change the syllabus.

Goodbye Yashika!

Teardrops are falling they're falling for Yashika
Our school and her friends have
tried really hard to save her.
But the home office; are sticking with their plans
They're hell bent on deporting her
they just don't understand
We've campaigned and we have
marched; but it's had no effect
Yashika we all love you; don't you ever forget.

She's gone back to Mauritius she's gone there alone
Yashika we'll remember you though you're far from home
Oasis academy Hadley is where you suppose to be
With your friends and teachers the Oasis family
So though we say goodbye we hope it's not the end
You'll always be a part of us our family and friend

Had A Girl

I had a girl some time ago we fell in love at school
She always said she loved me so I guess her love was true
But one April morning yes it was in the spring
When love supposed to blossom like
the daffodils and things

She said she wanted to leave me she had to say goodbye
I couldn't say a word I just broke down and cried

So now I do clubbing 2 or 3 times a week
I'm not looking for love just one night stands you see

So if you see me making eyes it's only for just one thing
Yeh pretty lady no love to you I'll bring
And if I ask you for a dance don't tell me that you care
Don't say to me you love me or want my love to share

You see I've been in love before so I guess I know the score
It can break your heart tear your life apart
It always make you cry when your love say goodbye

I don't want to be unkind but you
should know from the start
I don't want your love cos you might break my heart.

Halloween Night

It was the thirty first of October,
September had just passed.
The evening was dark and dreary, so
I decided to make a mask.

It's Halloween and everyone's going out,
they're going trick or treating,
On the corner of the street that's we're all meeting.

Knocking on doors asking for sweets,
if we don't get none then
We'll retreat.

Egging your house we may do that, or when
we flour bomb it, you'll hear "splat"
Running away were all laughing, we
just having fun it's entertaining.

Me and my gang we're walking the streets,
We're not looking for trouble we don't want no beef,
We're just having fun; having a laugh so catch
us if you can we'll give you a start.

In Loving Memory Rip Mrs. G

92 years you've been on the planet
We thank god for putting you on it.

Mother, Grandmother, Great Grandmother and a friend
We love you so much right to the end.

As you walk through the gates of heaven to him
You will see Mr. G he's been there waiting.

Sleep well Queen you will suffer pain no more
Standing by God's side; that's for sure.

Lazy

I like to sit and watch paint dry
I'm that kind a lazy guy

I like to sit and watch time fly
I sit and watch the clouds roll by

I don't move fast I move real slow
I've lost all my get up and go

Rushing around is not for me
Told you before I'm lazeeeee.

Man And Machine

Man make machine to do away with man
When we go shopping all we see a self-scan

Machine making machine to do away with man
There will soon be a day they won't need humans

Machine making machine to take information
Overloading of data might become a problem

Man making machine that can make cars
Machine making machine to fight long distance wars

Man making machine to do away with man
Machine making machine to supress humans

Man making machine to spot you from the sky
No more privacy for you and I

Mama Said

I should have listened to what mama said; she told me to
Beware
I should have taken heed to what mama
said; co.'s now I'm on my own
I'm afraid

She told me; you'd desert me boy, you'd
use me; treat me like a toy,
I never understood a word she said
co.'s love was in my heart
And it went to my head

That boy girl will use you and throw you aside
That boy girl will use you he'll take you for a ride

I never understood a word she said
co.'s love was in my heart
And it went to my head

I should have listened to what mama
said she told me to beware…
I should have taken heed to what mama said
co.'s now I'm on my own I'm afraid.

Mr. Babylon

Hey! Mr. Babylon let I go
Hey Mr. Babylon you hurt I so
You lock I up in captivity
Now you trying to rule with inequity
Let I go!

Do you class me as a rapist? Or a murderer
Do you class me as a arsonist or a burglar?
Let I go!

You trying to take advantage of me
With your sarcastic interrogation
Trying to make me look a fool
Taunting me bout repatriation
Let I go!

I must be cool I mustn't fight back
Cos you holding your truncheon
And might give me a crack
Let I go!

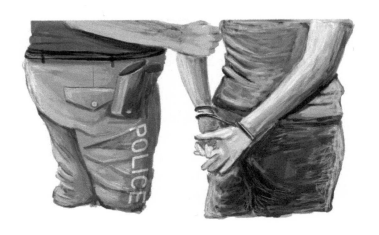

Nightlife In Soho

Sleazy nightclubs smoke filled bars
Attractive hostess's men with fast cars
Pushers trying to sell a pill
Hookers hoping to get their fill.

Neon signs go on and off
There is back street kids
Who dress like toffs

Explicit film shows showing the lot
Dirty old men getting hot

Nelson statue stands erect
His victory we will not forget
Theatregoers stepping out
From country town and all about

Buskers strumming to fill their tums
Then go back home to their slums
Police siren blaring loud
Searching for a face in the crowd

Sleazy nightclubs smoke filled bars
Bulky bouncers with razor scars
Pimps collecting their doe
That is nightlife in SoHo.

Black History

I was asked to write a poem
About someone black and famous
Someone who inspired me
Someone who was a genius

So I thought long and hard
Then came to my conclusion
It was quite hard so intense
So many to choose from

Mary Seacole, Marcus Garvey
Martin Luther King
Paul Bogle, Paul Laurence Dunbar
And Selassie I the king

So I decided with my intrepid mind
To look and try to find
On the internet I must see
Something about their pedigree

<u>Paul Laurence Dunbar</u>
Was the one for me, a man with fire and integrity

He was born of slaves in 1872
Dunbar was the family's name
Born in Dayton Ohio
His writing brought him fame.

He was the first African- American poet
To gain national and critical acclaim
His parents were so proud of him
He never bought them shame

He wrote his first poem at the age of six
At nine he gave his first recital
He also published his own work
He thought that this was vital

He wrote books of poetry
Books of short stories and a play
His works were published widely
In the leading journals of the day

To honor him they issued a stamp
And made his house a memorial
Dunbar rose to the top
His name is now historical

We should never forget that man
He was once a star
His name should never be forgotten
PAUL LAURENCE DUNBAR.!

Magpie

I saw a magpie in the tree; sitting there looking at me,
Wondering what he can get; but he is making me upset.

Cos if you see one they say it's sorrow,
I'll get prepared for today and tomorrow.

Now things are looking up; here come's its mate
Two mean's joy; and that I appreciate.

Looking out the window at the murky sky
Looking at both magpies as they pass by.

They look so calm they are at peace
Flying around with the greatest of ease.

Black Inventors

Black inventors on the internet is not hard to find
But they don't teach it in school so it's not in our minds

These great people should all be remembered
But they are not taught; why are they not considered?

We have traffic lights inventor and light bulb too
And did you know the blood bank was invented
by
Charles Richard Drew?

Thomas Elkin The modern day toilet,
Garret Morgan the gas mask and traffic lights
To name a few
Look on the internet you will see this is all true

Kell

Kind Eccentric Lovable Liked
He is quite loud but he is funny
Jumps around like a huge bunny.
Says he's got ways of making money.

Full of jokes and laughter,
We don't really know what he is after

Oh so energetic what
Does he eat? Not basic
Portions a whole lot of meat.

His temper is known
He goes crazy, hard to
Calm him down when
He gets in a frenzy.

Yes his name is Kell
He's not short
He's good in class
And he's very smart

The Exam Room

The exam room is quiet
We're told don't you say a word
But why is it so quiet
It seems so absurd.

The students are all on edge
Some look really scared
Some get panic attacks
And now their mind is impaired.

Maybe if they made it
Less solemn the students
Would be at ease
Right now they look like
They're been told they have
An incurable disease

Some are trying to rebel
By not taking part
But in the long run they're hurting themselves
And breaking their parent's hearts.

But seriously the exam board
Should make exam interesting.
The students are all scared and find it so depressing.

Macbeth

Macbeth at first he was a nice man
But for him the witches set up a plan,
Thane of Cawdor; yes you can,
They spoke in riddles and encouraged him.

He told his wife and she thought great,
Do what you have to do without debate.
Take your chance don't hesitate.

Macbeth had a friend called Banquo
A life friend he thought but woh!

Now Lady Macbeth said act like a man
Kill King Duncan yes you can,
When he comes to visit do the deed
This you must do to succeed.

Mac Duff found the King's dead body
Macbeth kill's the guard's and blame
Them for the tragedy.

Now King Duncan boys Donalbain and Malcolm
Both decided to go on the run, in fear of their lives
They both fled, we want to live don't want to be dead.

Macbeth is made King and things are great
Prophecies fulfilled but wait,
He starts to worry about the prophecy thing

He remembers the witches saying
Banquo son would be King.

He's now scared that he'll be dethroned
So he hires hit men to kill Banquo and his son,
Banquo is murdered but his son escapes
Things go downhill and Macbeth feels weird

He goes to the witches to hear what they say
More prophecy coming his way,

The latest prophecy comes in three parts
1) Watch out for Mac duff they start
2) No man born of a woman is going to hurt him
3) Don't worry until Birnam wood moves to Dunsinan
Macbeth breathes a sigh of relief again.

But the one about Macduff makes him worry
So he kills members of his family in a hurry,

Macduff and Malcolm visit the English king
Edward the confessor and started plotting,
They try to save Scotland from Macbeth
Who's so worried just sit and frets.
Lady Macbeth is not doing so hot in fact
She's lost the plot.
She dies of guilt Full stop.

When Macduff and Malcolm arrives with the
English army
They learned she had died and had gone barmy.

Macduff corners Macbeth and chops off his head
Alas Macbeth is dead.

The Bright Side

Optimistic that's me though my chances look slim
I'm a fighter and fight I will though the future looks grim

I'll take my chances one at a time and let them accumulate
for what you sow you must reap; one day it must be great

Chances are few and far between so I've got to have that
zest, to take whatever comes to me and try to do my best.

a pessimist; not me though my chances look slim
I'm a fighter and I'll fight to win
though the future looks grim.

Looking Forward

When I was younger my hair was black
But now I'm older its grey,
I can't fix that

You see with age you lose time
With time goes age; it's like reading a book
Going from page to page.

When I was younger yes my hair was black
So now I look forward; there's no turning back.

Young Playaz

I drive my car a don't drive no bus, when I drive
my car I cause nuff fuss, people look at me; and say
wow, dem try fe stop me; dem want a lift now.

So tuff luck if you need me, I told you let me be.
You do your thing I amma do mine,
I can't help it if I'm so fine

When I see girls, I go vroom; my
eyes pop out they just zoom,
Driving in my car;I feel proud, girls
everywhere shouting out loud.

A make money in all crazy ways; I'm a bad boy weh u seh?
In my ride making things happen; winner I am,
So i dare you seh sutting

We're writing bars we feel fine; words
flow from my lips all the time,
See a nice girl goanna mek her mine; my
world would end if a went blind.

my name is herb but a don't smoke; wen
people see me; they know I'm no joke.
Money in my pocket; a ain't broke,
I am the centre of attraction, just like the yolk.

When I see girls, i own the place; so be smart an gi me space
I am a man flying high; with all the
girls I get a don't need to try

As I said before I am the main man;
do what I want when I can
Said I drive a car no van; I cause nuff fuss cos I'm a don,

As you know I drive big tings; my
jewellery all day they bling,
I got haters and impersonators but they
copying me they imitators

Police on road wanna nick me what
can I say it's hard to be me
Always on my iPhone; so be a good boy and get my drone.

When I'm out click, click, paparazzi
chase me they want my pic

The Inclusion Room

The inclusion room is our domain, we
facilitate work to help them sustain,
a level of behaviour in the main a level
of education in the brain.
They fuss fight and complain; they
do this time and time again.
But we are there every day listening to what they have
to say, many have biased views some come in and
want to snooze while some are dazed and confused.

In this room we take action; though it may not be to
their satisfaction, all we ask; be responsible for your
actions better still try not to be sent to the inclusion.
We encourage and promote so please take
note, we're there for you always.
We aspire to achieve and yes we believe we
can make some difference to your lives

Shakespeare

Now Shakespeare was a man, who wrote Hamlet
He also wrote Romeo and Juliette.
He was a bard of the highest degree
He came from a middle class family.

Shakespeare was a man, who stepped up in life
From his middle class beginnings then he had a wife.
Ann Hathaway was her name, together
they enjoyed his fame.

Now he married her at eighteen in Stratford-upon-Avon

Shakespeare was a man with a lot of intellect,
Everything he wrote was coarperset

His plays were too numerous to mention,
plays about all kinds of situation
The Merchant of Venice, Hamlet and King
leer, Macbeth all had happiness and fear.

I Feel It

Eleven years since my Daddy passed
They said this feeling would not last
Yeh? Still I feel it, I feel it, I feel it.

My Mummy; she went soon after
No more songs no more laughter
Even more I feel it, I feel it, I feel it.

Now it's just me the boy and the two girls
Nothing left in our world
Yeh? We feel it, we feel it, we feel it.

Yes we know that life goes on
The three of us must be strong
But still we feel it, we feel it, we feel it.

Explanation

Scientifical explanation dem a try fe tell me seh, me
mentally disturb dats why me grow fe me hair dis
way, b'cause me hair is knot dem tink it's not ok but
I man kno me ancestors dem grow fe dem hair dis
way, so if u tink a joke go to school an learn it fe u self
go to de library study u culture tek it off de shelf

dem seh me abnormal an wen dem see
me; me seh dat dem squirm, tru me nu go
hairdresser fe go get weave and perm.
sometimes me happy sometimes me sad but most a de time
me proud cos over my horizon I can see no dark cloud.
cos i was born in Jamaica of Jamaican family mi
mother mi father mi sister come yah in a sixty three
dem settle down and work and further more dem book
mi passage and send fe me in nineteen sixty four
dem sen me go to school archway secondary,
mi only leave archway wit two CSE mi but
me went and study in a higher degree
wen mi leave school mi go work in a factory, weh mi
put me money? Building society; mi nah keep it a yard
man sake a robbery, de yout dem now a day's dem nuh
av no money, dem we bruk ina u house intrude pon u
privacy tek what's not theirs sell it an mek money.
But I man Mr. Herbie seh dats not de way to be
go to school get a job elevate from poverty.

Wen I was a yout dem call me Junior tru me
av de same name as me father but now I am
a man dem call me Herbie seh everybody call
me herbie! seh everybody call me herbie!

Albany Close Oasis Open

I lowered my head and wore a frown
When they said Albany school was closing down
But a bright light shone in my face
The vision of Oasis taking its place

The format the ethos it was all new
A sense of direction had come into view
A new uniform which the students chose
A new school will open while the old one close

Some teachers have left not giving it a chance
They've gone back to India, Africa and France
Teachers have left from math's and drama
Not aware Oasis could have been their karma

Students now look refreshed and bright
We're moving forward and it's such a delight

"Same students "I hear it'll still be the same
I say give it a chance don't out the flame

Aspire, Achieve, Care Endeavour is our light,
This we hope will help us shine bright.

A Leaving Wish

We're sorry to know that you're leaving
Good luck and all the best,
This is now your future
The second part of life's test.

You may be studying further
May be you are looking for a job,
But whatever your aims are
Don't let it be a slob

All those years you've had in school
You had good days and bad,
And now that you're leaving
Everyone is really sad.

Well take care and do your best
Believe in yourself! Don't cry,
Your future lies ahead of you
Make the most of it; please try.

Family Feud

I'm caught in the middle of a family feud
If I say my piece they say I'm rude,
I'm walking on eggshells
Don't want them to crack; they won't be
happy till I'm lying on my back.

I'm caught in the crossfire of a family feud
I must say my piece excuse me for being rude,
I'm on the outside looking in I've got to say something
so let me begin.

I'm caught in the middle of a family war
Trying to clear the obstacles but they're raising the bar

Some say they hate me; I'm trying to keep out
But my girl's in the war zone I got to help her out

Won't raise no white flag or carry no arms
The weapons I'll use will be supportive and calm

I'm caught in the middle of a family show
They all want to be the star I'm just
watching from the back row.

Family Life

Living with my family is hard I must confess
fussing and fighting- unhappiness
My daddy wants his own way he can't see I want mine
my mummy is a go between; a referee all the time

He tries to treat me like a youth but I'm a full grown man
he don't want to face the facts he don't want to understand

Because I live under his roof I must do as he says but I
am an adult now, so somewhere else I'll find to stay

Living with my family is hard I must confess
fussing and fighting unhappiness

Guilty

Guilty now you'll have to pay;
Guilty no don't runaway
I've found you guilty for misusing my love
I've found you guilty my sweet, sweet love

Nothing is perfect in life so now that we're man and wife
Let's give it a go, give it a go
Let's give it a go, give it a go

Complaining and moaning fussing
and grumbling cannot help
Cheating and beating fighting back biting cannot help

Nothing is perfect that I've seen so now
I'm your dread and you're my queen
Let's give it ago, give it a go
Let's give it a go, give it a go

Guilty now you'll have to pay; guilty no don't runaway
For trying to put me down guilty treating me like a clown

"Summarise"

I don't get demoralised; I am stabilised
So I don't really socialise.
I tell the truth; I don't tell lies
I visualise and memorise.

If I can't specialise
I improvise
How I save my money? I capitalise.
Though I capitalise
I don't privatise.

To keep good time; I synchronise
To keep in shape I exercise.
I'm non judgmental I emphasise
I don't criticise or victimise.

I'm not bad I don't vandalise;
Because the good Lord I immortalize.

Working with children I specialise
I get abused but myself I immunise.
I don't use drugs nor tranquilise; I
am very clean; I sanitise.
As a role model I try to epitomise; and act civilised
I must carry on or; I could become immobilised.

Just Because

Just because someone want to use and abuse me verbally
It doesn't mean when they're ready I must smile.

Just because you hate me and you want to manipulate me
And you say sorry; I must try?

Just because you want your way, so you don't have to pay
That won't register in my mind.

Pressure in my head; but it's not something you said
I don't know if I'm coming or going.

Leave me alone and let me reflect
On the thoughts in my head
I will not change or rearrange my principal's
You know; I'd rather be dead

Just because someone wants to verbally
or intellectually abuse me
It doesn't mean when they smile I'll smile

Look Back

They reminisce of yester year those rocker-Billy's that's
who, of songs like tutti-frutti and also blue suede shoe

They admired Gene Vincent, James Dean and Elvis P,
They adored Jean Harlow, Monroe and Cyd Charisse

They loved to jive all the time especially in their drapes
They loved the beat they stomp their
feet when they are in their crepes

Bill Haley said good-bye to his alligator, Buddy Holly died
premature those days of yesterday, are gone for evermore

Look What You've Done

You must really hate me to give me the sack co's
you broke my heart and now my hearts cracked
To mend my heart here's what to do just come
round in person but don't bring no glue
I'll always love you I know I will, don't need
no prescription don't need no pill

Together we planned ahead, the world
was our oyster now all that is dead
Maybe it happened co's you wasn't sure,
but I am hurting and I'm feeling sore

Perfect for me in figure and form, you use to hold me
and keep me warm you're head it was good you had it
screwed on, but now you won't tell me what I did wrong

Did I really hurt you did I make your life hell?
Compare me to others then come back and tell
your children come first of course i know that;
Did I ever hurt them? I think that is crap.

I gave them more than I got, is that not the facts
what did they do for me let's talk about that
think of yourself and your future needs, there's a
man who loves you and his heart now bleeds

Sometimes I think and I wonder why, how did it get
to this stage? should I just lie and say it was me?. It
was my entire fault; but I know it wasn't - so I won't

My Views

The human race is disturbed
With politicians making our vision blurred.

People in authority they have the upper hand
Telling us things we don't understand

The world is starving but still they make bombs
To sell and to kill each other; then they add up their sums

They are in power; but they don't really care,
They don't help those who are in despair.

They say war is imminent
But why must it be?
Let's love one another for prosperity.

Politicians making war the public
They want peace
Talking about their neutron bombs
And their foreign policies.

Redundant

I've been made redundant and I am feeling blue
I've been made redundant yeh that's true

For years I've worked here with nothing to show
I've been made redundant now I've got to go

Can't pay my light bills, I can't pay my rent
I can't pay my HP's my money's all spent.

Places to go to, friends ask me out
I've got to say no; can't afford my shout.

I've been made redundant now that makes me sad
three million unemployed now that makes me mad.

Show Me What To Do

Hey! Valentino, show me what to do
I'm in love with a princess but I just can't get through
You used to be a charmer; all the girls were after you
So tell me Valentino tell me what to do.

Hey Casanova give me some advise
Tell me what to do when I'm with her tonight,
You see I get all tongue tied and tremble like a leaf
I don't know what to do I always come to grief.

Should I buy her flowers and take her out tonight?
Or romance her with music under stars so bright?

Tell me Valentino how to use my charm,
When you're with a woman you always looked so calm
Should I be forceful with her will that be alright?
What shall I do when I'm with her tonight?

Don't be afraid

Don't be afraid it's only hair, come talk
to me don't stand and stare
Don't give me a smile and then wonder,
is he alright or is he a mugger?
Don't be afraid it's only hair, come talk
to me don't stand and stare.
I could be bad I could be good; do I need to prove myself?
Do you think I should?

Don't be afraid give me a chance, get
to know me before you advance
What's on your mind what's in your head? Am
I interesting or do you want me dead?
Don't be afraid give me a chance, get
to know me before you advance
Maybe I'll help you maybe I won't, please don't judge me
I beg you please don't

I grow my hair long that's how I like it,
don't be afraid please don't resent it
It's only a hairstyle is it scary to you? I
won't say sorry co's I don't have to.
Don't be afraid it's only my hair; I see
you're bald but I don't care
Don't be afraid its only my hair, come
talk to me don't stand and stare.

My Life

I'm sixty years old and I'm stable; God
knows I'm still willing and able.
The years have flown by at the blink of an eye,
I'm no more young, free and single.

My life is good, I'm happy. In school, I was always chatty.
But I had respect, intelligence and zest.
And a good circle of friends around me.

When I left school, I thought I was a man,
I really didn't even have a plan,
But I never walked with any gang.
Too much respect for my fam.

Studied in college, along with working,
Put my head down, no skylarking,
The future, I'm embarking
Legit ways to make money I'm embracing.

1975 I had a little girl, best thing
ever happened in my world.
A beautiful daughter, who I never scold.
Made me so proud, if the truth be told.

I was happier than I'd ever been,
My parent's first grandchild, on the scene,
We thank you lord for this lovely gene.

Now I'm older and well matured, I
look back on my life, I explore
All the good times I want more, I'd
do it all again that's for sure.
Getting old don't make me sad I'm sad because
I lost my mum and dad
My heart beat and the light of my life
That cut through me like a knife.

But I'll carry on in their name and for myself
To ease the pain
I don't expect to amass much wealth
I accept the hand I've been dealt

I'm <u>HAPPY</u> and <u>CONTENT</u>
For all the things I represent I work hard
For not much money but the key words for me are;
<u>CONTENT</u> and <u>HAPPY</u>

A Wish For My Sister

Thou you're overseas I feel I must extend
My best wishes to you as your brother and friend
You're thought of very highly even
when you get on my nerves
The way you live your life I look and I observe

So it gives me great pleasure and for me to say
Keep being nifty now you're sixty
Don't let age get in your way.

Those Days

Oh I wish for those days when we were all friends
When we were all boys trying to be men
Oh I crave for those days when we were in school
And the girls used to rate us; oh yes I do

We had manners and we showed respect
To the elders of our community elect
Not confront them direct

Oh I wish for those days

Times were hard but we had fun
No mobile phones or posing like Dons
Oh I wish for those days of time gone by
Oh yes we were hard but we didn't hurt a fly

Oh I wish for those days when prices were low
Any money we had was spent in Chapel market
Or Walthamstow

We would be out playing football till ten or eleven
That was our idea of Heaven

THOSE DAYS

The Mirror And Me

I look in the mirror and what do I see?
I see me in there looking at me
I stop pause and I ponder
Is that how I really look? I wonder

I look in the mirror and what do I see?
The person in there is looking at me
Why am I thinking like this? It's just a reflection
But does he exist?

Some People

Sometime you're good to people and yes they're good back
But then they upset you now you're on the attack
They don't like that

They look at you as though you are evil
Even proclaiming that you are a devil
They expect to see the good in you all the time

But they're not showing it though
So you tell them what; what,
And what to do with themselves
But they don't like that.

Age

Age is just a number take it as it is
Age is just a number use it as a positive.

Someone I love was born today

Wishing you a wonderful birthday

I am wishing a happy birthday
that is a special in everyway

May your special day have many excitement fun and appreciation.

Wish you to love life and never stop dreaming

May beauty and happiness Surround you today and always hope you have the happiest birthday

You deserve everything that you desire So make your birthday wish And let it fly higher

Happy Birthday

You are thought of in a very special way, and your wished the finest things in life.

Wishing you a happy

Wishing you many happy return birthday.

of the day

xxxx

May your birthday be filled with the warm Sunshine of love.

Hope you have a fantastic day.

xxxx

May all your wishes come true.

Best wishes for a Wonderful birthday.
xxxx

57

57 years I've been on the planet
I thank my mum and dad for putting me on it
I give thanks and praise to the lord above
For showering me with all this love

My eyes are open so I can see
The world is round and I'm free
Born in Jamaica of Jamaican family
Jones town Kingston originally

1964 first time on a plane
Heading for England to see my folks again,
I'm in two minds; happy and sad, I don't know
Just want to see my Mum and Dad

8 years old I don't know what's going on
It's freezing cold and there's no sun
I'm going to school I'm learning fast
My first school play and I'm in the cast; as Joseph

Years have flown they have gone by quick
I'm starting secondary school I think that's the lick
I am trying to be a good boy to make them proud
I want to stand out from the crowd.

The NHS

Jeremy Hunt what is the problem with the NHS?
It seems there's a lot wrong It's in a right old mess
I tell you Jeremy mate I've just sat in A&E
I just don't understand it it's really puzzling me

The time I sat and waited made me so distressed
It made me feel worse than when I came in
There was no happiness

The NHS used to be so good
Kind efficient and calm
Now there are hardly any doctors or nurses
That's why there is such an alarm

Jeremy Hunt what is going on?
Why does it take so long?
A&E is not very fast they're weak
Yet they used to be so strong

We sit around in A&E some even fall asleep
I cannot see this getting any better
In fact it is quite deep
You think your name is about to be
called then your hope is dashed
When they walk by you want to cry and
something you want to smash

Snow!

When I woke up this morning all I saw was snow
Beautiful, white all a glow
The sunlight had made it all crisp
Careful how you walk it is easy to slip

No lightening no thunder it just came nice and calm
Flickering down on my manicured lawn
It came with a whisper no thud or no bang
Just falling down all over our land.

Happy!

I am happy I'm happy I'm sad no more
I am happy I'm happy and here's the score
Look on my face you'll see a big grin
I'm happy outside and also within

I'm confident and having fun
I'm doing alright
I'm confident and having fun
The future looks bright

When I see people I give them a smile
Being happy is my style
My mojo's back I'm on the go
No more sitting down or lying low.

I Loved You

I met you after school and got to talk to you
I told you how I felt, but then my heart began to melt

Co's I loved you and needed you from the start

We were going together strong,
But then something just went wrong
Now you're going to walk away,
And how I pray for you to stay

Co's I love you and I need you don't ever part

Girl you had control of me
But I was just too blind to see
Now you said you've found somebody new
Look how you've gone and made me blue.

Many a sat day nights I sit at home and cry
Yes I'm thinking about you baby
And how you drive me crazy

Co's I love you and needed you from the start
I still love you and want you back in my heart.

Charities

Every year about Christmas time
They put adverts on TV
Asking us to send money
To different charities

We'd all like to do it
Yes we would of course
But which one should we choose
The abandoned dog charity
Or home for the beaten horse?

There are water aid charities
And children of Syria too
There are homeless people at crisis
But what on earth do you do?
These adverts have got me all perplexed
Yes I'm very confused
I'm in such a pickle now
So I just refuse.

Getting Old

I'm old now I'm over sixty when I was young I was nifty
I use to play football sports of all sorts
But now my body I can't contort

Pains in my joints killing me
But something in my head keep telling,
You can do this you can do that
But a whole lot of agony I'm feeling

I'm old now I'm over sixty when I was young I was nifty
A athlete yeh I loved to race, but now
I'm older I have no pace
And my cartilage has decreased without trace

When I was young I use to party
Now the future with these joints scares me
When I was young I'd play all sports
But now my body I can't contort.

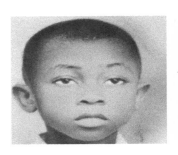 

You're More Than

You're more than I ever imagined
You're more than a woman to me
You're more than I could have hoped for
And I'll love you endlessly

You're always doing things for me
You make my life so sweet
And when you say you love me
You make my life complete

Yes you're more than a woman you're magic
You're an angel in disguise
And when I say I love you
Stars twinkle in your eyes

When I was young I dreamed of
Someone exactly like you
But I never thought that one day
My dreams would all come true.

Yes you're more than I ever imagined
You're more than a woman to me
You're more than I could have hoped for
And I'll love you endlessly

My Prayers

I pray to the Lord I ask above what is this thing called love
I try to find without success; a love
that will bring me happiness

Sometime I sit at home and cry; Asking
the Lord, the reason why?
I give love yet suffer so; I always end
up with nothing to show

I ask the lord to show me the way to
love, to work, to rest and play
to have a future free of vice; yes my soul I'll give to Christ

My heart has love; my mind has doubt,
But the Lord and I will work it out.

<u>In God I Trust!</u>